I Know Someone Who Uses a
Wheelchair

Sue Barraclough

Heinemann Library
Chicago, Illinois

www.heinemannraintree.com
Visit our website to find out more information about Heinemann-Raintree books.

To order:
☎ Phone 888-454-2279
🖳 Visit www.heinemannraintree.com to browse our catalog and order online.

Edited by Rebecca Rissman, Dan Nunn,
  and Catherine Veitch
Designed by Steve Mead and Joanna Hinton Malivoire
Picture research by Tracy Cummins
Originated by Capstone Global Library
Printed in the United States of America by
Worzalla Publishing

14 13 12 11 10
10 9 8 7 6 5 4 3 2 1

Library of Congress Cataloging-in-Publication Data
Barraclough, Sue.
  I know someone who uses a wheelchair / Sue Barraclough.
    p. cm. — (Understanding health issues)
  Includes bibliographical references and index.
  ISBN 978-1-4329-4567-1 (hc)
  ISBN 978-1-4329-4583-1 (pb)
  1. Wheelchairs. 2. People with disabilities—Orientation and mobility. 3. People with disabilities—Transportation. I. Title.
  RD757.W4.B365 2011
  617'.033—dc22   2010026583

Acknowledgments
We would like to thank the following for permission to reproduce photographs: age fotostock pp. **13** (© Jeff Greenberg), **14** (© Jochem Wijnands); Alamy pp. **17** (© Photofusion Picture Library), **20** (© Howard Barlow); AP Photo p. **27** (Jane Kalinowsky); Corbis pp. **7** (© Jim Sugar), **8** (© Andersen Ross/Blend Images), **10** (© Andersen Ross/Blend Images), **11** (© A. Huber/U. Starke), **23** (© Mika), **26** (© Charles W. Luzier/Reuters); Getty Images pp. **6** (David Handschuh/NY Daily News Archive), **16** (Zigy Kaluzny), **19** (Jim Cummins), **21** (Jamie McDonald); istockphoto pp. **15** (© Egidijus Skiparis), **18** (© technotr), **25** (© Franz Pfluegl); Photo Researchers, Inc. pp. **4** (Olivier Voisin), **24** (LADA); Photolibrary p. **22** (Imagesource Imagesource); Shutterstock pp. **5** (© Varina and Jay Patel), **9** (© Tatiana Belova), **12** (© prism68).

Cover photograph of a young woman in a wheelchair playing tennis, Maui, Hawaii, USA reproduced with permission of Photolibrary (Superstock).

We would like to thank Ashley Wolinski and Matthew Siegel for their invaluable help in the preparation of this book.

Every effort has been made to contact copyright holders of any material reproduced in this book. Any omissions will be rectified in subsequent printings if notice is given to the publisher.

All the Internet addresses (URLs) given in this book were valid at the time of going to press. However, due to the dynamic nature of the Internet, some addresses may have changed, or sites may have changed or ceased to exist since publication. While the author and publisher regret any inconvenience this may cause readers, no responsibility for any such changes can be accepted by either the author or the publisher.

Contents

Do You Know Someone Who Uses a
    Wheelchair? 4
Why Use a Wheelchair? 6
Living with a Wheelchair 8
How Does It Feel? 10
Different Types of Wheelchairs 12
Moving Around 14
Staying Healthy 16
Keeping Active 18
Wheelchair Sports 20
Being a Friend 22
What Can I Do? 24
Famous People 26
Using a Wheelchair: True or False? 28
Glossary 30
Find Out More 31
Index 32

Some words are printed in bold, **like this**. You can find out what they mean in the glossary.

Do You Know Someone Who Uses a Wheelchair?

People use a wheelchair for lots of different reasons. Some people use a wheelchair because they do not have legs, or their legs do not work. Other people use a wheelchair for part of the day because their legs get tired.

Some people use a wheelchair because their legs are not strong enough to work.

Some people who use
wheelchairs cannot walk,
so they use a wheelchair
to move around.

Some people who use wheelchairs
have had an accident that damaged
their legs or **spine**. They may need to
use a wheelchair while their legs and
spine are healing.

Why Use a Wheelchair?

Some people who use a wheelchair have a **disability** such as **muscular dystrophy** or **spina bifida**. Muscular dystrophy is when the **muscles** become weaker and weaker, and then stop working.

Wheelchair users are just the same as you and have the same interests.

People with a disability can still take part in many sports.

Spina bifida is when the **spine** develops differently. Many people with spina bifida cannot walk. They use leg braces, crutches, or a wheelchair to move around.

Living with a Wheelchair

Moving around in a wheelchair can be difficult sometimes. Many things such as light switches and door handles are in places where a person in a wheelchair cannot reach them.

Automatic doors help a person in a wheelchair to move around.

Specially designed features, such as ramps, help wheelchair users.

A person who uses a wheelchair needs to learn how to move around in lots of different places. Some stores and offices have ramps to help people who use wheelchairs. You may have noticed other **features** to help wheelchair users in buildings and streets.

How Does It Feel?

Imagine how it would feel if you could not go to certain places.

Just like everyone else, people who use a wheelchair feel happy when they can move around and do the things they want to do. Sometimes they feel angry or sad that they cannot move around easily.

Everybody needs friends to understand and **support** them. Nobody should feel left out.

People who use a wheelchair may be teased, left out, or bullied because they are different. Always tell a teacher or an adult if you hear somebody being teased or bullied.

Different Types of Wheelchairs

Wheelchairs can be light, fast, and easy to use.

Some people use a very light wheelchair that makes it easier for them to move around. A small, light wheelchair can be moved easily and lifted in and out of cars.

Many wheelchairs have lots of **features** to help a person get around and do things. These wheelchairs have to give **support** for the body as well as move quickly and easily.

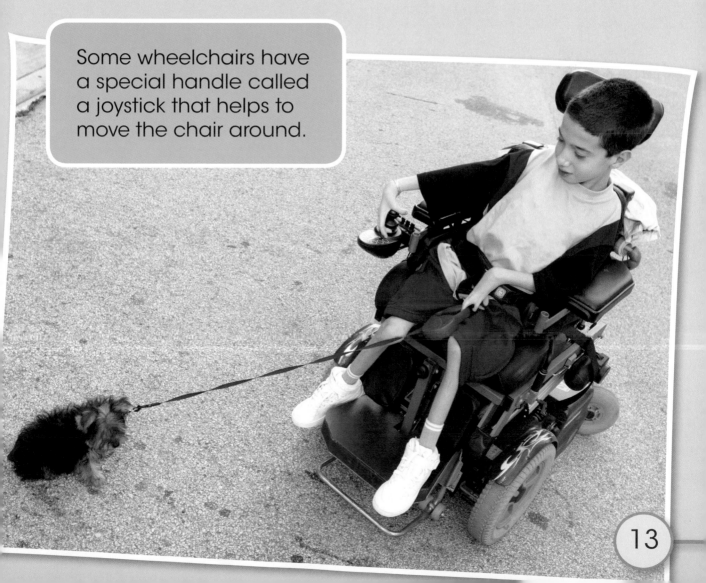

Some wheelchairs have a special handle called a joystick that helps to move the chair around.

Moving Around

A wheelchair is important because it allows people to be **independent**. This means they can do things for themselves and do not always need help.

A massage can stop **muscles** from getting stiff and sore.

A wheelchair user needs to learn to control it safely and well.

People who use a wheelchair can learn a lot from a doctor or **therapist** about moving around. They can also find out about new ways to do daily tasks, such as washing or getting dressed.

Staying Healthy

Food and drink keep your body working well. It is important for wheelchair users to eat a mixture of healthy foods to keep them fit and strong.

Food gives our bodies energy to move, grow, and keep warm.

Some gym equipment is specially made to help wheelchair users keep fit.

It is important that wheelchair users find out how to make working **muscles** stronger and discover new ways of moving. Keeping as active as possible is a good way to stay positive and happy.

Keeping Active

Strong arms are important for moving and controlling a wheelchair.

People who use a wheelchair need to keep their bodies fit and healthy. Exercising every day helps to make the body stronger and more able to do things.

It is important to do a mixture of games and activities every day to stay fit. Wheelchair users may need help to do some activities, but it is important that they stay active and healthy.

Wheelchair sports are a great way to stay fit and healthy.

Wheelchair Sports

Just because people use a wheelchair does not mean they cannot play different kinds of sports. There are many sports, such as basketball and tennis, in which wheelchair users can play as part of a team.

Basketball is a popular wheelchair sport.

These wheelchair athletes have won medals at a sports event called the Paralympics.

Some wheelchair users become great athletes. Many wheelchair users work hard to do well in certain sports. They need strong arms and stomach **muscles** to move their wheelchairs fast.

Being a Friend

A person in a wheelchair usually does not need to be pushed around, but there may be other things you can do to help. Do not forget to:

- always ask if help is needed
- be thoughtful—for example, a person in a wheelchair might need more space to move around
- listen to instructions about how to help safely.

You can help by reaching for things that someone in a wheelchair cannot reach.

Friends understand that wheelchair users want to find things out for themselves.

Understand that a person in a wheelchair may take a little longer to do some things, so try to be patient. People who use wheelchairs want to be able to move around and do things for themselves.

What Can I Do?

Help your friend to find activities that a person in a wheelchair can join in with. You could do the activity together. There are many organizations that give wheelchair users the chance to do exciting activities and sports.

The Internet is a good way to find out about new clubs and activities.

People in wheelchairs want to make friends, just like anyone else.

People in wheelchairs do not want people to feel sorry for them. They want to be treated the same as everyone else. Wheelchair users want to live life, have friends, and be happy.

Famous People

Stephen Hawking has an illness that affects his brain and **muscles**. He cannot walk, talk, breathe well, or swallow, and he has difficulty holding up his head. His wheelchair helps him do these things.

Despite his **disability**, Stephen Hawking is a world-famous scientist.

On July 13, 2006, Aaron did the first wheelchair back flip.

Aaron Fotheringham has **spina bifida**. When he was born, his mother was told he would never sit up. But Aaron crawled. Then he walked using leg braces and a walker, and then with crutches. He started using a wheelchair when he was eight and has been doing stunts at skate parks ever since.

Using a Wheelchair: True or False?

All people who use a wheelchair need help to move around.
FALSE! Most wheelchair users can move around by themselves.

People who use wheelchairs can drive cars.
TRUE! Many wheelchair users are able to drive cars.

All people who use a wheelchair are sick or sickly.

FALSE! Many people who use wheelchairs are very healthy.

All people who use a wheelchair cannot walk.

FALSE! Some people use a wheelchair to take a rest from other ways of moving around. Many people who use a wheelchair have had an accident or operation, so they need to use a wheelchair as they get better.

Glossary

disability illness or injury that makes it difficult to do some things

feature important part of something

independent not wanting or needing help to do things

muscles strong, stretchy body parts that are attached to bones and that help us to move

muscular dystrophy condition that affects the muscles and makes them weak

spina bifida condition in which the spine grows differently. The spine is not protected properly, so a person with spina bifida often cannot stand and walk.

spine part of your body that carries messages between your brain and other parts of your body

support hold up or help

therapist person whose job is to help sick or disabled people

Find Out More

Books to Read

Powell, Jillian. *Sam Uses a Wheelchair* (*Like Me, Like You*). Langhorne, Pa.: Chelsea Clubhouse, 2005.

Royston, Angela. *Using a Wheelchair* (*Young Explorer*). Chicago: Heinemann Library, 2006.

Schaefer, Lola M. *Some Kids Use Wheelchairs* (*Understanding Differences*). Mankato, Minn.: Capstone, 2008.

Websites

http://kidshealth.org/kid/
Visit Kids' Health and type "Wheelchair" in the "Search here" box to learn more.

Index

activities 7, 19, 24

bullying 11

cars 12
crutches 7, 27

doctor 15
door handles 8
doors 8

exercising 18

food 16

gym 17

joystick 13

leg braces 7, 27
legs 4, 5
light switches 8

muscles 6, 14, 17, 21, 26
muscular dystrophy 6

offices 9

ramps 9

spina bifida 6, 7, 27
spine 5, 7
sports 7, 19, 20, 21, 24
stores 9

teacher 11
tired 4

walk 5, 7, 27, 29